HOW I LOS
IN 3 WEEK

CW00515036

By Anthony Grant

My name is Anthony Grant and for the last 23 years I have been practicing an energy psychology called Rone Therapy at lifeenhancers.co.uk

Until I was 55 years old, I had always been

ill. I was born during the second world war, and arrived with eczema and jaundice. At 18 months old I had asthma.

I was sent to a convalescent home at the age of 5 until I was 10. I was institutionalised.
I was very insecure through most of those 55 years.

They say that childhood asthma will

leave every 7 years. It left me 8 times that when I was 56 years old.

I have since found that asthma is caused by insecurity. Hence the 7-year cycle. A child of 7 might become secure in their life, or at 14, or 21 etc.

So at 56, after an extremely varied life, I felt secure. It was because I went on to develop Rone Therapy, which is the most advanced talk therapy in the world.

Getting and keeping others well ever since has been my life, and this little book is another step.

How I lost 2 stone (28lbs) or 13KG in 3 weeks, and I didn't even realise it was happening.

This is not a why and wherefore chat, this is a very simple, easy to understand and **satisfying diet** that always works on nearly everybody (there are always exceptions to any rule) without causing discomfort in any way.

Being overweight, can mean one of two things, you are eating the wrong foods, or insufficient exercise, or both. I was always around 10 stone for the first 55 years of my life, but then the pounds started rolling in. I went up to between 11st 7lbs and 12 stone, not good for me.

Then about 4 years ago, after reading two good books, I decided that what I had read made sense. I had to change what I was eating, and get some more exercise.

The result shocked me, as I went from 11st 7lbs (73kg) to 9st 7lbs (60 kg) in 3 weeks without any adverse effects.

I was amazed how simple it was and to be honest, I didn't set out to lose weight, I just set out to become healthier, and didn't realise until my trousers were falling down, so I weighed myself. I had lost a stone (6.3 Kg)

I had researched earlier, that if you cannot see your collar bones because of the excess flesh, or you are carrying weight below your belly button, the problem may be that your lymphatic system is not working as it should. (this is very common in the over 50s)

The lymphatic system is the body's waste disposal system. It does not have a pump like the heart, it works by movement of the cells/you. If it's blocked, not only do you put on weight by keeping the body's waste, but many other things could and generally do go wrong in the body.

So how do you make this lymphatic waste

disposal system work as it should? The simple answer is – exercise. There are many different types of exercise, but being lazy, the only ones I used were a rebounder (mini trampoline) and a stepper.

You can also visit a lymphatic masseuse. Lymphatic massage is a very nice way to get the lymphatic system moving, but I chose to do it myself through exercise.

Now I'm not into exercises. I spent the first 55 years of my life as a chronic asthmatic and allergic to the 20th century. In the last part of those first 55 years I had arthritis in my hips, so you can see, any kind of exercise caused my breathing to suffer, and severe pain in my left hip.

When I was diagnosed with arthritis in the early 90s, the surgeon asked if I was an athlete, or did I do a lot of running. I asked "why do you ask?" Well you have severe arthritis, it is a waring disease. I replied "That cannot be right, I have the least worn hips in the world, I don't run anywhere, I walk as little as I can.". He replied with "it's a nice day today "

That set me to think about my arthritis and realised in the late 90s that arthritis is initially caused by negative emotions. I went on to say, "98% of everything the body suffers from, starts with a negative emotion". That is another story. One day they will figure it out.

Exercise

So I was very adverse to exercise, but the stepper and trampoline are easy. The trampoline is the best way to get your cells activated. Dormant cells don't work very well, so why do cells have to be worked?

Our bodies are continually replacing itself, In a year 90% of our bodies are replaced by new cells. Each tiny cell is a manufacturing plant replicating itself.

Two simple things to see yourself replicating are your hair which grows around 1cm per month, and your fingernails at 3mm per month.

Your skin is replaced every six weeks, your liver replaces itself every 2 months. 100 million red blood cells are replaced every minute, your skeleton replaces 10% of itself per year and so on. The only things that stay with us are our eye lenses and central nervous system. And how about this, fat cells take 8 years to replace,

If all this replicating is going on, it becomes quite obvious that the body can only replace itself from what we eat. If we eat rubbish; we get rubbish cells, so we are what we eat.

Now the cells can only work efficiently if they are acted by movement, any sort of movement, which in my case was as little as possible. The cells have to be compressed which is what happens with movement, so you can see why the mini trampoline is ideal for compressing cells. 1-300 jumps a day is all I did.

In order to keep my muscles working, I went on my stepper: doing 2 to 3 hundred quick short steps in a minute or so, a few arm exercises with push ups at my desk, and that is my total exercise regime.

I, like many of you, thought I had a good diet to start with, but I couldn't lose any weight. What I couldn't lose was my waist and my waste. My lymphatic system was not working properly, but now I had the exercise worked out, I looked at my food.

One thing I had done for the last 40 years was eliminate most saturated fat from my diet. I never ate fat on meat, never used butter only spreads, I only used vegetable oil to cook with. I never drank milk. Anything I thought had fat in it, I wouldn't eat.

I had been told by our health system that saturated fat increased my cholesterol and I was at risk of having a heart attack, so I had to keep my cholesterol low. You all probably do the same. The only fat I ate and didn't realise it, was egg yolk in eggs.

My cholesterol level was 7, and at the time was ok, then they moved to 5 and wanted to put me on statins. No thank you, I've had 60 years doing ok at 7, so I'll decline your offer.

My Normal Diet

There is a saying that the Italians live to eat

and the British eat to live. I am one of those who eat to live. As a man, I am habitual (not so with women) I can have the same meals over and over for weeks, and then change as my fancy tells me to.

My original diet was as follows:

Breakfast,

1 had a poached organic egg, a couple of heated tinned tomatoes and a slice of brown bread with a rapeseed oil-based spread. To me, it tasted better than butter. Followed by a cup of green tea with a spoonful of honey.

Mid-morning, a slice of toast with spread and honey, again with a cup of green tea and honey.

Lunch

Lunch has been my main mealtime, because we have the greatest amount of stomach acid earlier in the day. The acid declines in the afternoon, and by 6pm, there is very little left. People who eat late into the evening are rarely hungry in the morning, because they have only just started digesting last night's meal. (mostly "A" blood types. That's another story)

So for lunch I used to have a fair-sized portion of meat, beef, lamb, chicken or turkey, with steamed vegetables consisting of sprouts, runner beans, broccoli, organic carrots and sweet potatoes, covered with thick Bisto gravy again followed by a cup of green tea and honey.

Mid-afternoon, some tinned fruit and soya-based yogurt with a cup of green tea and honey.

Tea

For tea I had an organic egg on toast, sometimes with baked beans, or fish and tomatoes, or toasted cheese and tomatoes, a slice of bread and spread, again followed by a cup of green tea and honey.

Supper

For supper I had a small slice of cake and a couple of biscuits, yes you've guessed it, followed by a cup of green tea and honey.
I also took, a 50billion pro-biotic, 1000mg

vitamin C, 30mg Boron, one drop of Lugol's iodine in a glass of water once a day and 500mg calcium with magnesium, zinc and vitamin D3 (one tablet) twice a day.

That was it day after day. I never drank water. I just didn't like the taste.
Then I changed, but as you'll see, not by that much.

My New Diet

My new diet includes saturated fat. **Eating saturated fat does not make you fat, it makes you slim.**

Don't stop reading if you disagreed with that statement, I shall explain.

I was shocked when I first read about it and this is what I read and commented on.

There are many types of fat, but we only know about the ones that are in the supermarket. There are the vegetable oils and spreads that sound good and safe to eat. Let us take the most common, rapeseed oil. We've all seen the fields of yellow flowers producing an amazing crop for the farmer.

Rapeseed oil was originally made to lubricate heavy engineering, but then vegetable oil manufactures started looking at making it a consumable. It had everything going for it, it grew very easily, it never had to be sprayed with insect repellent because the insects wouldn't touch it and it was very cheap, so they refined it.

This process includes caustic refining, bleaching, and degumming – all of which involve high temperatures or chemicals that are damaging to the human body. Last but not least comes the deodorization process that turns it into a trans-fatty acid, which

is one atom away from plastic.

All oils that are not cold pressed go through the same heat process. The best cold pressed extra virgin olive oil, and extra virgin cold pressed coconut oil are the only oils that should be used in cooking and **these fats are essential for our wellbeing**.

I eat 3 table spoonful's of coconut oil every day.

T he body uses the oil and fats to make our cell membranes. If you make a cell membrane from near plastic oil, the cell won't be able to take in the glucose it requires for replication.

The unabsorbed oil/fat is moved away for storage in the body as waste, and cannot be called upon for energy at a later date. So if you have been eating takeaways or ready meals that are cooked in vegetable oils, it's the wrong sort of fat, it's the one which puts on weight.

So for your health's sake, only eat cold pressed olive oil and coconut oil, or real animal fat. Avoid rapeseed oil if you can, because as you will see, rapeseed oil is in most edible products you buy. If we don't buy the bad oils, they won't make them

If you are talking about fat, then you have to talk about cholesterol.

Cholesterol is, as far as your doctor is concerned, (Doctors only tell you what the big pharma has told them.) a big problem today. If you have a cholesterol reading higher than 5, your doctor will tell you that your risk of having a heart attack or stroke is 50% greater if you do not take statins. That is quite a statement, and frightens people into taking them, but where did your doctor – big pharma get that statement from?

From a physiologist named Dr. Ancel Keys. He published nearly one hundred papers from 1985 to 1995 while he was at the University of Minnesota.

One of Key's studies started most doctors believing that the more fat you eat, the more likely you are to have a heart attack. Big pharma who employed Keys, went on to produce a money-making cholesterol-lowering drug called statins.

Some of Key's trials said that there was a relative risk of 50% of having a heart attack or stroke without taking statins, and that was what the doctors were told by the drug companies. The problem is that doctors are too busy to read all about the trials and generally only read the summary or just listen to the drug rep who comes every month to sell their drugs, so what is this frightening "relative risk of 50%?"

Risk.

I thought, as you probably think, is that all risk is absolute, but in the pharmaceutical industry risk is assessed in two ways, absolute risk and relative risk. I can only think they use relative risk to frighten you in to using their drugs.

Absolute risk is when you have two groups of test people. One group takes statins, the other a placebo. At the end of the trial, 2% of the statin group had died of heart problems compared to 4% of the placebo group. So **the**

absolute risk is the difference between the two results which is **2%.**

Relative risk is the relation of one result to the other. 2% is 50% of 4% so the relative risk is **50%.** 50% more people died in the group that did not have statins, and that is how drug companies use the figures. Your doctor heard "The relative risk is 50%, but your doctor was unaware what relative risk is.

We also know from Key's revelations that the groups of people he chose in his trials were biased in favour of using statins. Statins do lower cholesterol, but it has now been found they do more harm than good. He also said that saturated fat was the cause of high cholesterol as it could enter the arteries. It was Key's research that led us all on to the path that fat was bad for us.

As you know there has for many years products advertising "low in fat". It is the wrong fats that cause the problem.

The liver makes cholesterol, it makes as much or as little as the body needs. If you have a high cholesterol reading, it is because the body is trying to clean the liver, so do yourself a favour and clean it yourself. (There are many internet articles on liver cleansing.)

The last thing you want to do is to reduce your cholesterol by taking statins.

Now I hope you understand why saturated fat is a very

necessary part of any diet, but is included in none except my new diet.

Incidentally, Keys stated after he left the employ of big pharma, **that there was no way saturated fat could possibly enter the arteries**.

New diet

Breakfast.

For breakfast I had two poached organic eggs (or boiled, fried in coconut oil, scramble etc.) - (or one if you wish, or other protein to match) and a slice of bread covered with lots of goat's butter, (saturated fat) followed by a cup of warm water and a table spoonful of coconut oil. (Saturated fat)

Mid-morning,

At mid-morning I had some fresh fruit, a banana, or pink grapefruit, (eat more if you want) followed by a cup of warm water.

Lunch

For lunch I had a very small portion of meat, (2 to 3 ounces.) of beef, lamb, chicken or turkey, (omit if you are a vegetarian) with steamed vegetables consisting of (as much as you want) sprouts, runner beans, broccoli, organic carrots and sweet potatoes (no other potatoes) covered with Bovril gravy, (or stock if you don't eat red meat) followed by a cup of warm water, and table spoonful of coconut oil.

Mid-afternoon

At mid-afternoon I had some fresh fruit, grapes, a banana or pink grapefruit, followed by a cup of warm water.

Tea.

For tea I had the same as breakfast, two poached organic eggs (or some fish) and a slice of bread covered with lots of goat's butter followed by a cup of warm water and table spoonful of coconut oil.

Supper,

For supper, a cup of warm water.

The main differences are, **I am eating a lot of saturated fat,** a very necessary commodity in any diet, because it satisfies the hunger pangs you get with other diets (or so I am told) and only drinking warm water. A little warning here, don't exceed the three spoonful's of coconut oil a day, if you do, (I did) you may like me, end up with gout, and that is painful.

After three weeks I had lost 2 stone. If you

carry on, you will lose more weight.

So what are you eating, 4 organic eggs a day. Protein

Two slices of bread. Carbohydrate

Goat's butter, (Cow's butter is ok, but not from the fridge butter, that contains rapeseed oil Check it.) Saturated fat

Fruit and vegetables. Mostly carbohydrate.

Organic cold pressed coconut oil. Saturated fat

And I only drank warm water. Warm tastes very different and is better for the body.

I also took daily and still do,- 50 billion pro-biotic,- 1000mg Calcium with magnesium,

Vitamin D3 – 1-2 grams vitamin C powder, and 500 mg of marine phytoplankton which supplies all the rest of vitamins and minerals my body needs.

There are some who find that eggs make them constipated. If that occurs, start taking vitamin C powder (ascorbic acid) A level teaspoonful is 4 grams.. Start with 2 grams and double it every day until your bowels work, and they will. You cannot overdose on vitamin C.

And that is how I lost 2 stone in 3 weeks, but for me there was a problem. When you get to my young age of 75 and lose that percentage (17%) of fat/waste, because the collagen production has slowed to near zero, my jowls dropped and I looked haggard.

People were asking if I was ok? My neighbour thought I was very ill. So I simply went back to the tea and honey, twice a day, porridge occasionally in the morning, a piece of apple pie and maple syrup mid-afternoon and a biscuit for supper, and I have put on a stone and half. 7 pounds less than when I started, and that suits me fine, but see how easy it is to put on weight!

Add a little of your favourite food to keep the same weight. Remove it when you start gaining too much weight.

· Now if that isn't simple, tell me what is. If you have a problem changing anything, or have no will power, come and see me. With Rone Therapy you can change your taste buds or thoughts or feelings or ………. Look me up at lifeenhancers.co.uk

At this time of writing, I am now 79, I still have 3 tablespoonfuls of coconut oil, eat 2 to 4 eggs a day, jump on my rebounder and use my stepper every day. I am as fit as I have ever been, and my muscle tone is excellent.

My rest heart rate is 58bpm, The biological age of my arteries is 60

If you don't look after yourself, one day you will realise that with all your wealth and possessions, **without your health, you have nothing**.

I hope you find this to be the simplest diet you have ever tried, and one you continue with. **Please review this book**, as very few people realise that eating saturated fat is a very necessary protein to keep you well, and it keeps you slim. And remember, before the advent of vegetable oils in the 1970s, there were very few overweight people.

Now you know why.

Printed in Great Britain
by Amazon